Cowboys & Critters

Symbiosis in the American West

Nebraska cowboys, cattle and horses
Texas cowboy Troy Reinke working for the Haythorn Ranch in Arthur, Nebraska. © Charles W. Guildner

"A horse! A horse! My kingdom for a horse."

William Shakespeare, 1564-1616,
"Richard III"

Let it rain!
Tim Malsam of Chinook, Montana, still manages a smile through heavy hail, rain, sleet and snow on the Hofeldt Ranch near Lloyd, Montana.
© Todd Klassy

PUBLISHER/EDITOR: C.J. Hadley
LEAD WRITER: Carolyn Dufurrena
ART DIRECTOR: John Bardwell
STORYTELLERS: John Bardwell, Virginia Bennett, John Dufurrena, Linda M. Hasselstrom, Bill Jones, Robert Laxalt, Rene Maestrejuan, James Ployhar and Vess Quinlan.
EDITORIAL ASSISTANT: Ann Galli
PROOFREADER: Denyse Pellettieri White

Publication of this book was made possible by generous donations from people who care about the American West.

No part of this book may be reproduced in any form or by any electronic or mechanical means, including information storage and retrieval systems, without written permission from the publisher, except by a reviewer who may quote passages in a review.

Library of Congress Cataloging-in-Publication Data
Hadley, C.J.
Cowboys & Critters
Caroline Joy Hadley
ISBN 9780964745674
LCCN 2016946658

Published by Range Conservation Foundation & RANGE magazine, Carson City, Nevada.
All rights reserved.

$45 U.S.A.
Printed in China
Copyright © 2016 Range Conservation Foundation & RANGE magazine

Close encounters
By C.J. Hadley

RANGE magazine, which co-published this book, has been an advocate for cowboys and sheepherders for a quarter century. Its writers have covered issues that threaten the rural West and the good people who live and work there. This includes endangered species, wetlands, takings, government regulations, urban encroachment, and innocent newcomers who have the money to buy huge ranches for the view but little understanding of how to keep them healthy.

Some environmental activists and academics want to remove all livestock and the people who tend them on our western ranges. They prefer a buffalo commons to a multigenerational functioning symbiotic and productive community. One group's mission is to acquire "the largest nature reserve in the continental United States." Its followers believe that enormous parks will protect the creatures that inhabit them—but only if the families who have sustained that land and kept it thriving and beautiful for generations are no longer there.

Most agree that precious resources should be used in a sustainable way. If grass is not eaten it becomes decadent and dies. The result is bare ground which holds no moisture and provides no forage or cover. Ranchers who work this land have experience not found in books but from generations of knowledge handed down. They are out there every day and see firsthand that nature can be cruel. They know they must protect the resources and use them well or their families and the wild and domestic creatures that depend on them will not survive.

The photos and stories within these pages are of the cowboys and critters that share these western ranges. Most live in harmony, all with respect, and some—like dogs and horses—with great affection.

Mule deer fawns © Larry Turner

Wolves © Joe McDonald/Tom Stack & Associates

Snowy owl © Diane McAllister

> "In Westerns, you were permitted to kiss your horse but never your girl."
> Gary Cooper, 1901-1961

CONTENTS

Outside the fences 8
By Carolyn Dufurrena

The clever coyote 20
By Vess Quinlan

Buster's horses 26
By Carolyn Dufurrena

Calf CPR 36
By Virginia Bennett

First generation sheepherding 46
By Carolyn Dufurrena

Bilko 52
By Bill Jones

Ground squirrels 67
By Carolyn Dufurrena

Forty field hands for the noon meal 70
By Carolyn Dufurrena

Mustangs 74
By Tim Findley

Buckaroo
Matt Rice brings in the cavvy for the Whitehorse Ranch, Steens Mountain, Oregon.
© Larry Turner

Great egret
Tenmile Lake, Oregon. © Larry Turner

Antelope baby lunchtime
© Andrea Tolman

Great horned owl 81
By Rene Maestrejuan

A truly durable joke 90
By Vess Quinlan

Decades of protection 97
By James Ployhar

The raven 109
By John Dufurrena

Science lesson, Dog River school 116
By Carolyn Dufurrena

Whirlaway: A shot of used grass 126
By Linda M. Hasselstrom

Critters or varmints? 133
By John Bardwell

Love 'em or hate 'em 134
By Carolyn Dufurrena

A tree frog in winter 140
By Carolyn Dufurrena

The shaming of the cat 156
By Robert Laxalt

There's something about a redhead

Yearlings line themselves up for a photo on the Mulvey Gulch Ranch in Boulder, Montana. © Annie Branger

Horses & cows

Horse's mane
Sunset at the WB Ranch in
Grass Valley, Oregon. © Cathy Brown

Outside the fences

By Carolyn Dufurrena

Living on the land means living more with animals than people. Some we care for, some we watch through field glasses as they meander through our world. Some appear in our yards, in our bathrooms. We learn to permit their presence in ways that our urban cousins do not appreciate. Some animals we nurture, some we curse as they lay waste to our plans for field or irrigation ditch. But

Your horse is your ticket to solitude and community, both commodities increasingly rare in this world. The horse gets you out into the great wide landscape, for as long as you can stand it.

Heading for the pasture
Quinn River, Nevada. © Linda Dufurrena

animals can always be trusted to be exactly what they are. They are not duplicitous. They do not lie. They think in their own mysterious ways, some brilliantly.

The cattle, the sheep, the dogs that work for us, and the ones who sleep in the sun, their working years long past, are animals under our care. We have a certain relationship with them. The saddle horses are a different story. They're colleagues. Co-workers.

Temple Grandin, world-renowned expert on autism and animal behavior, says: "Riding a horse isn't what it looks like: it isn't a person sitting in a saddle telling the horse what to do by yanking on the reins. Real riding is a lot like ballroom dancing or maybe figure skating in pairs. It's a relationship."

Every horse has his own personality, his own quirks and foibles. There are things that make him crazy: a white rock in the sage, a tight draw where he can't see. Still, he'll take you wherever you need to go, as long as you respect him and don't act like an idiot.

Your horse is your ticket to solitude and community, both commodities increasingly rare in this world. The horse gets you out into the great wide landscape, for as long as you can stand it. He carries you to your work, and your peace. That horse brings you to a community of comrades, working in big outside country. The camaraderie of work done together in the middle of nothing but sky and grass is some people's idea of heaven.

One day at branding, a big strapping kid came to help: competent, for sure, but more farmer than cowboy these days, married into a life "inside the fences." He was a little bit bored with that life, you could tell, and maybe that horse was too. The bald-faced sorrel took him far up the draws and across some big country getting to the branding trap. In a long, dusty day, 170 head of big calves were branded. That big kid's horse pulled his share of calves, working alongside all the other horses. Later that afternoon when they were finished, the kid grinned a crooked grin and asked, "Now what, Boss?"

The boss said, "Put 'em all back. Right where you got 'em." He got a blank stare from the kid for a minute, then a laugh as the boss said: "No, we'll kick 'em out the north gate. They'll find their way

Nose
Daryl and Bobbie Mitchell of Cleveland, Montana, rope cattle on branding day on the Malsam Ranch near Chinook, Montana. © Todd Klassy

up the mountain." The kid swung up on the bald-faced sorrel and rode out; they both looked happier than they'd been for a while.

Horses are not pets, no matter what some folks want to believe. Sensitive and intelligent, they do not think like people, in spite of our deepest wishes. Temple Grandin says that our biggest mistake with animals is to imagine that they do. We anthropomorphize, tell ourselves that we know what motivates them. This is simply not true. We diminish them by pretending.

We share our world with all these creatures, wild and domestic, in a world increasingly less wild. Our world is more engineered, more regulated than ever, the rules stipulated by urban dwellers who do not understand the flow of life across these ranges, but attempt to govern all actions, to preserve a snapshot in time: this many sage grouse on this hillside, that many grizzly bears in that mountain range. They attempt to model and calculate and predict a pattern in a complex web of patterns that are incompletely understood, a pattern that

will change with the next range fire, with the next flood, with the next hard winter, the next virus.

Man believes he is in charge, and believes regulation is another way to conquer the natural world: we will protect the wild creatures. We will mandate this, we will regulate that, and we will be the ones in power, not Nature. And Nature laughs at us. "Make your studies," she says. "Draw your boundaries, build your fences. Protect your ravens and your eagles, and watch them eat your precious sage grouse. Protect your grasses from grazing, and your forests from harvest, and watch me burn them all. Watch me make a mockery of all your plans."

We humans are too slow. We are not clever enough to change. We should be more humble.

The animals adapt magnificently, though their world seems as if it will never recover. Hard squalls in summer rake the soil from the hillside after fire; sheetwash brings floods of rock and gravel down the canyons. Snowberry, bitterbrush, the sage and lupine and shooting-star columbine become part of an imagined landscape in the season after wildfire. The habitat map drawn so carefully in some office two years past is transformed by that devastation and the snow of the following winters; yet the sage grouse return, perhaps thicker, to new grass growing in the meadows, the rank, overprotected plants cleared, if not by grazing, then by fire.

The mountain rebirths itself, its sharp contours softened with junegrass, fescue, bluestem, foxtail, paintbrush. Willows return. Young aspen

A tasty morsel
A bald eagle followed a golden eagle to feed on this coyote. © Patricia Neely

reach into the sky, thick groves revived, feeding the deer that lop the tender shoots, hiding the creatures that stalk those deer. One wet winter gives the grove the boost it needs to recreate itself, to shelter the

Hundreds of antelope
Pronghorn herd watches the photographer in remote northwestern Nevada. © Larry Turner

mint, the wild iris, the hemlock, the small animals beneath. They all adapt.

Adaptive behavior: sage grouse nest in short sage at a rural airport. In the midst of all the federal hoopla, a neighboring rancher states that the birds fly "over the highway, out of the junipers, between the power lines, across the field and over my barn, and nest in the meadows a half-mile from the airfield by the hundreds." Though alarmists fear the airport noise will keep them from settling, think of it another way: the ravens might just be scared of the jet wash as well. Coyotes might give a wider berth to the planes and the people who might shoot them. There's a reason the sage grouse continue to nest at that airport.

The fact is, we merely share this country with the wild things: with the ground squirrels that dig holes in the yard, with the frogs in the bathtub, with the snakes that curl in the cattle guards and stretch across the road, hunting mice and small rabbits. The beavers in the creeks gnaw away at the fence posts and pile willows under the bridge, yet they build the ponds that enrich the meadows and raise the water table. They're part of our world too.

Coyotes and bobcats prey on housecats and calves. Lions and bears take deer, lambs and young horses. Mares come in from summer range scarred by long stripes, claw marks on their flanks where they've evaded the cougar. A few every summer sacrifice this year's foal.

Antelope birth their kids under the sprinklers for safety, nestle their young in knee-deep alfalfa. They will hide from hunters in those fields in autumn. Deer cache their fawns in the willows and in the same deep alfalfa. The hay crew will halt their big loud machinery and climb down to move the babies into a windrow, out of harm's way. The deer melt away into the meadows and the thickets, but emerge the week before hunting season, seeming to know no one will be allowed to shoot them, at least not legally, in those fields. They will winter in the yard, sheltered from the coyotes and the north wind, cleaning up the apples in the orchards and the last of the fall leaves piled against the fences.

Stewardship does not just mean care of the land. It means recognizing the rich and complex world of wild things that inhabits this land as well. Coexistence may not be easy; but we learn it by living this life, on the edge of the wildness, with the creatures that live here.

Protection

Always watching
Great Pyrenees with lambs.
© Diane McAllister

Wolf in search of prey
© Robert S. Michelson/Tom Stack & Associates

Bobcat
Photographed from a kayak while paddling the Wood River, Fort Klamath, Oregon.
© Larry Turner

Fine-tuning burro
© Diane McAllister

"Real freedom lies in wildness, not in civilization."

Charles Lindbergh, 1902-1974

Song of the West

Raven
Ever the opportunist and much like the coyote, ravens adapt well to almost every environment and situation. Depending on circumstance, they may be predator or scavenger but are always ruthless.
© Alan Hart

Devoted cowboy
Checking calves during a wet spring storm on the Sargent Ranch near Shawmut, Montana.
© Kayla Sargent

Efficient hunter

This red fox mother in southwest Wyoming had eight kits and brought food to the den as often as every fifteen minutes. I watched her drop a dead bird out of her mouth to catch another bird out of the air. She left the food at the entrance to the den, and a kit would come out and grab it and run before a sibling could take it away. Truly survival of the fittest. © Tammy L. Hoover

Rattlesnake

© Scott Linstead/Tom Stack & Associates

Desert bighorn

Walker Lake, Nevada. © Sheree Jensen

How's this for natural camouflage?

The clever coyote

By Vess Quinlan

The phone rang just as Leo, the boys and I had finished lunch. Our hired man Leo was more a member of the family than an employee and was lecturing the boys, Norlan, twelve, and Justin, ten, about how important it was to stay with the sheep they were herding and not go off hunting rabbits.

Albert Luster, our neighbor to the north, had called to tell me we were losing a lamb a day to a coyote when the boys came home for lunch. She had dug under the fence and as soon as the boys left in their pickup the old coyote would grab one.

Albert was irrigating his alfalfa field and changed the water every day at about noon. He saw the coyote one day and meant to call me, but his phone was out. When he saw the coyote slip under the fence the next day after hiding in the brush and waiting for the boys to leave, he figured he better let us know she was a regular visitor.

"That's a pretty smart coyote," Justin said. "How does she know when it's noon?"

"Coyotes don't have watches," Leo said. "She has been watching and knows boys and pickups mean guns, so she waits for you to leave. She is killing sheep so is probably old and has been shot at before. If she is getting a lamb a day, I'll bet she is feeding a den of pups and they will all be sheep killers."

"I hate to kill her," I said. "But we can't afford to let her have a lamb a day. One of you boys is going to have to lie in a ditch with your rifle where she can't see you while one of you leaves in the pickup and shoot her when she comes under the fence. Maybe the government trapper can track her back to the den and deal with the pups. I don't like the idea of leaving them to starve."

"Boy that makes me mad," Leo said.

"Why, Leo? That coyote is just trying to make a living for her family just like we all are."

"I wasn't talking about the coyote. I was thinking about Mr. McPherson."

"Why are you still mad at Mr. McPherson? Hell, he's been dead for thirty years."

"Mr. McPherson brought three thousand ewes and lambs to run on Wild Horse Mesa. It was the war, Boss, and almost everyone was gone fighting with the Japanese and the Germans. The priest told Mr. McPherson that I was pretty good with sheep so he hired me to herd them. I was fourteen and tried really hard, but it was a mess. Mr. McPherson gave me these two lazy dogs. Those dogs were stupid, Boss. They didn't know nothing about sheep and they were cowards. When the coyotes came around, they hid under the camp and whined.

"He gave me five boxes of shells and this rifle that was so heavy I had to lay down to aim it. I shot up all those shells and did not kill one single coyote. I think the barrel was bent. Those coyotes were laughing at me. I'll bet they told each other not to be afraid of that kid, Leo, he makes a lot of noise but he never hurts anybody.

"Those coyotes ate a lot of sheep that summer, Boss. When we counted them that fall, Mr. McPherson was really mad. He said, 'Well that proves one thing, Leo. It proves that coyotes are damn sure smarter than Mexicans.'

"If that Mr. McPherson were still alive, I would knock on his door and tell him that coyotes are smarter than gringos too."

Coyote looking for its next meal
Yellowstone Park, Wyoming. © Pamela S. Wickkiser

I'm watching your backs

An Akbash sheep dog moves a flock of sheep at Julie Hansmire's Campbell Hansmire Sheep Ranch near Eagle, Colorado. The big white dogs have been bred for centuries to bond with the sheep and guard them from predators. © Kathy McCraine

Feeding the leppies

Linda Dufurrena bottle-feeds the orphan lambs. Some years she has more than one hundred at the Dufurrena Ranch in Denio, Nevada.
© Larry Angier

Future guardians of the flock
© Chrystal Sims

Dairy bar

Carson City, Nevada. © Diane McAllister

Guiding him back to Mom
During the fall gather at Winnemucca Ranch north of Reno, Nevada, this little guy got left behind.
© Debbie Bell

Buster's horses

By Carolyn Dufurrena

Perhaps his first horse was a dog, at least one likes to think so, a burly long-haired border collie, or a rangy Catahoula, that he could curl his small two-year-old fists into, and ride around the yard beneath the cherry trees.

The next mount a mule, either Pat or Charley. By the age of five, he was on his way to sheep camp up the canyon with his cousin, to while away the afternoons with the camptender, fishing in the little creek and following along as the old Basque made his circle through the sheep camps scattered across the ridges.

Soon old enough to ride the seven miles down to school in Denio, he'd stable his steady horse in the old rock barn across the road, and then ride home after class. When the weather got bad and the days were short they'd drive him; his father would make a free hour to get him down to town.

A buckaroo horse was next, to carry him, so young still, on a man's work day, across the valley, around the point to the hay meadows twenty miles distant, following the steers to summer pasture. Carry him home, back across the long valleys all the long way that afternoon, stopping in Denio with his older brother, sleeping on a chair in the bar while listening to the talk of war. Riding the rest of the way in the dark, back to Wilder, under the stars.

Then the wild buckers and mustangs of young manhood, horses hard to ride, with unexpected fits and starts that would throw a guy headfirst into a greasewood, horses they didn't start till they were five years old. The horses were ready for the tough work they'd have to do, but you'd better be ready, too, they said. He was part of a crew of young men those years, brothers all. They rode everything, and proved everything they needed to prove.

Later on, with work to do, he rode a tall strong long-walking horse, one that could outwalk a lesser beast trotting alongside, ride out before daylight, go all day through the rocks, brand when you got there, and walk all the long miles home, day after day. They were tough horses, tough men to ride them. Years of that, riding for the work he loved.

Later on, less time spent horseback as the demands of the ranch increased; then he gathered up mares to raise the colts that would grow into horses strong enough to carry men all day and gentle enough to carry his grandkids, that's what he was after.

His last horse was a swather. He rode up and down the meadows and alfalfa fields, his dog in the cab, his grandson swathing beside him, still trying to keep up, the old man not hurrying but going steady, steady, for hours and hours, sometimes. He'd stop for lunch, but the kid would skip the meal, or eat in his machine so he could catch up to where the old man was. In recent years, he would stop sometimes at the end of a windrow, just for a few minutes, and have a little nap before rousing himself and going on again.

And now at last, released, he's going away at a long trot across the valley and into the hills he loved. He'll hold up there on the other side, wait for us to catch up one day.

"There's nothing better for the inside of a man than the outside of a horse."

Ronald Reagan, 1911-2004,
40th American president

El Poeta Dream
Buster rode a lot of horses, but never one of these. The Peruvian Paso was bred for plantation owners of South America. It might be the kind of mile-eating smooth ride he'd appreciate, though. This stallion belongs to Barbara Windom of La Estancia Allegre in Alcade, New Mexico. © Ozana Sturgeon

Desert tortoise
Always taking it slow. Always worried about predators, like ravens, coyotes, raptors and heavy-booted humans. Always looking for the fresh, moist, protein-rich droppings from the cowboys' bovines. © Larry Angier

Gophersnake
Glossy after shedding its skin and with a testy temperament, this critter is sometimes called a bullsnake and mistaken for a rattlesnake. © Alan Hart

Black-tailed jackrabbit
Also known as the American desert hare, a jackrabbit's ears can be seven inches long. Ideal prey, its only protection is to run very fast—up to forty miles an hour. © Larry Turner

Critters that live close to the ground

Burrowing owl
Solano County, California. © Diane McAllister

"Predators glide silently above on friendly air currents. They carefully stalk in the grass and brush. Their prey, always vigilant, stay low. Very low. Under the radar."

John Bardwell

The work of a season: Northern Plains

This far north, calving season begins in April, and the work of branding runs from June into August. Cows and their calves graze in outside country until fall, when most are old enough to leave the mother cows. A sea of black, this herd of Angus cattle heads for winter pasture near the Canadian border in early November. They will stay on grass until the snows come.

Learning them early
Gabe Clark, cow boss of the Grindstone Ranch in Daniel, Wyoming, is branding a calf while holding his son, Jak. Jake Wolaver is holding the heels. © Skye Clark

Sea of blacks
Black Angus cattle move to winter grassland in November, Olsen Ranch, east of Whitewater, Montana. © Todd Klassy

"The voice of that country is an open whisper, pointed at intervals by the deep whir-r-r-r-r of the sage hens rising from some place of hidden waters. Times when there is moonlight, watery and cold, a long thin howl detaches itself from any throat and welters on the wind."

Mary Austin, "The Flock," 1906

Mingling
Pronghorn antelope in sage grouse lek near Honey Lake, Lassen County, California.
© Diane McAllister

Nevada mule deer bucks

Mason Valley. © Tammy L. Hoover

King of the hill

Rocky Mountain bighorn sheep battle at the north fork of the Shoshone River near Cody, Wyoming. © Willie Felton

Looking for work
Oman and Patch greet the photographer from the back of the truck at a branding near Valley Springs, California. Most of the time Stan Dell'Orto's dogs only get to watch the action. © Larry Angier

Ready to play
Not allowed to work during branding, Craig Joses' dog Zoey keeps amused by continually fetching a stick at the Joses' outfit in Calaveras County, California. © Larry Angier

> **"The dog was created especially for children. He is the god of frolic."**
>
> Henry Ward Beecher
> 1813-1887

"Every dog must have his day."
Jonathan Swift, 1667-1745

I'll take care of you
Wesley and the puppies at Red Barn on the Wooster Ranch in Calaveras County, California. © Larry Angier

Calf CPR

By Virginia Bennett

I knelt on the icy ground, coatless and shivering. It was February 1993 on a cow/calf outfit not far from the Canadian border. A few moments earlier, I'd spied an old cow off by herself, frantically circling a limp calf, then stopping to lick it with long strokes of her rough tongue. At other times, she gingerly nudged the dark form that had just slipped out of her womb and into a frigid and cruel world.

Her calf was a monster: big-boned and dark gray. I'd already rubbed his wet hair with my gloved hands while I prayed for his life. Although his eyes presented a sightless stare that never changed, even when my finger touched his lashes, and even though I failed to detect any breath coming from his nostrils, I just couldn't accept him being dead. I wrapped the big calf in my coat, carefully tucking much of the insulated material between his cold body and the ice. In that high-mountain valley of north-central Washington, ranchers breed their cows to calve in the first two months of the year so that they are big enough when it comes time to make the grueling trip up the steep trail with their mothers, bound for alpine meadows and summer grazing.

Taking a stiff-armed stance and placing my hands, one palm upon the other, behind the elbow of the calf's right forearm, I began steady compressions. Solitary flakes of sleet drifted from the muted sky, landing on my coat as it swaddled the calf. Opportunistic ravens waited for a chance at the afterbirth. Although I'd never heard of anyone giving mouth-to-mouth resuscitation to a newborn calf before, it wasn't hard to figure out. Lifting his face off the ground a bit and turning it toward me, I plugged one nostril with my right thumb while holding the mouth closed with my left hand. I next completely covered the left nostril with my lips pressed against slimy, chilly nasal tissue to form an airtight seal, and blew in forcefully.

My improvised method seemed to be doing what I intended, so I continued the strong breaths of air from my lungs into the lungs of the calf. Snow settled on his beautiful face and eyelashes. But I also noticed something unnerving: each time I blew into that nostril, the calf's right eyeball (the only one visible to me from that position) rolled back into his head. When I took my mouth away and my breath drifted out from his lungs, the eye would return automatically to its previous blank stare. Over and over, with each one of my breaths, his eyeball rolled back and then returned forward. At times I'd stop briefly to make more compressions over the calf's front ribs, but my best motivation came from seeing the movement of that eye.

After several more breaths, I stopped and silently studied the calf's nostrils, and soon I was rewarded with the sight of a very faint fluttering, the slightest sign of the calf coming to life and trying to breathe on its own. Very tenuous and faint. I held my own breath and watched.

Eight months later, I watched the ranch's weanlings (including that stout gray calf) trot up the ramp into the semitrailer. The absentee owner, whose name would appear on the sales receipt and check made out at the livestock auction in Okanogan, would never know of the classic struggle of life and death that occurred on his calving grounds the previous winter. But Pete and I sure enough recognized that calf which, like all the others on that truck, had survived the summer, grazing with their mamas in the remote high country of the Pasayten Wilderness.

Saving that calf didn't make us a dime more pay and it sure didn't bring any glory. We were just doing what all good ranch workers do, regardless of the hour of day or night, in spite of extreme weather and unaffected by weekends or holidays. It was the right thing to do.

Licking the baby clean
Cow No. 322 nudges and bonds with her newborn calf at the Stoney Creek corrals of the Busi Ranch in Amador County, California. © Larry Angier

"Houston, Tranquility Base here. The Eagle has landed."

Neil Armstrong, July 20, 1969

Good feed, a lovely view
Sandhill cranes fly over farm wheat leaseland at Lower Klamath National Wildlife Refuge. Mount Shasta, California, looms in the background. © Larry Turner

Strutting for the girls
Sage grouse male flashes for the females at a lek in Red Gulch, Big Horn County, Wyoming. © Marion Dickinson

America's symbol
The bald eagle.
© Larry Turner

Helping hand

Bart McCollum and daughter Olathe get ready to go for a ride on Hoss in Rozet, Wyoming. © Caitlyn McCollum

Buddy and Tyler Joy
Buddy's mom didn't survive a rattlesnake bite so he came home.
© Debbie Bell

Concentratin'
Billy DeLong competes in the young buckaroos reining class at the county fair in Elko, Nevada.
© David Kimble

Shipping time

Tim Wilbur gets his rope ready to catch a calf at the Winnemucca Ranch north of Reno, Nevada. It's in the wrong pen. © Debbie Bell

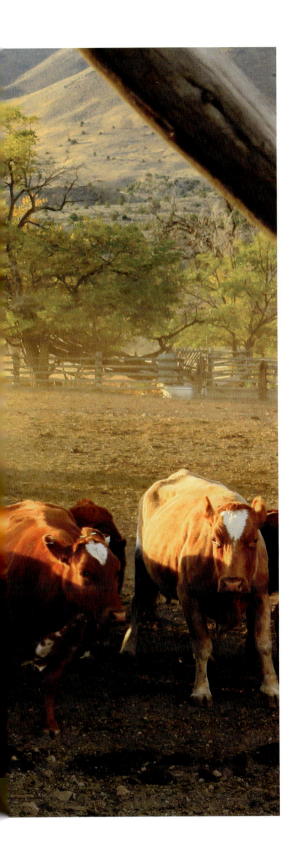
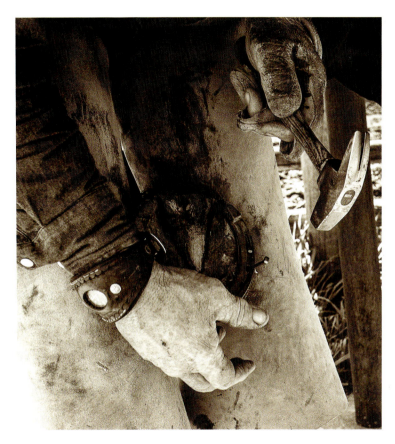

Nailing iron

Ken Clark nails shoes on his saddle horse. He has shod equines for fifty years, often twenty or more a day. Clark Ranch, Smoot, Wyoming.
© Skye Clark

"Animals are such agreeable friends—they ask no questions, they pass no criticisms."

George Eliot, aka Mary Ann Evans, 1819-1880

Kindness is what the world needs
© Linda Hammond

Connections

Real cowgirl

Kassy Brough of Havre, Montana, rubs the soft nose of her horse on a ranch outside of Bozeman, Montana. © Todd Klassy

If only we understood them

My little brother and his friend Hezekiah enjoy a chat on the Mendenhall Angus Ranch near Celina, Tennessee. © Rebekah G. Mendenhall

First generation sheepherding

By Carolyn Dufurrena

He celebrated his twenty-fourth birthday alone in the winter sheep camp, down on the desert where snow covered low-growing sage. The ewes muttered in the vast gray silence, and he watched the two-rut track to the north, waiting for the camptender. Three days, four. Another snowstorm, heavy and wet, crusted the ewes until the world was many shades of white: the buff-white ewes, the white sky, the white of the mountain, the blue-white of evening. He waited in the white silence, all through his birthday and beyond.

The camptender came on the fifth day. The sun had broken through, softening the roads, bringing color to the desert: the dark green-gray of the twisted sagebrush, the red and black of the hulking mountain above him, the brilliant sky. His family had been coffee farmers in Sonora, Mexico. They were a family of many brothers, too many for the small farm. It was time to move, make another life in the north. So Miguel had slipped across the border, in the path of an elder brother, and found this job herding. He had stuck with it for a couple of years. When the loneliness of sheepherding became too difficult, he would follow his brother one more time. He would learn to mechanic for the big farm in Dog River Valley, over the mountains to the east.

In a few years he would bring his wife and their two boys to live on the big farm. There was plenty of work. The brothers slipped one at a time into the valley, and then soon their wives, and children.

Sheepherder in the Sierra
Border collies help move the band and big white guardian dogs help protect them from predators. © Sandy Powell

Teamwork
Five border collies work alongside and are good company for the herder as he brings ewes and lambs to the corral. © Cindy Quigley

Coming home
Pregnant ewes are guided to the home ranch until lambing, F.I.M. Ranch, Yerington, Nevada. © Jon Hill

Stand back, let's see what happens

This North American porcupine in Dillon, Montana, was trying unsuccessfully to hide in a low scrub tree. My rancher friend, Don Reese, volunteered to lightly poke it with a stick so it would turn toward me. We were relieved to confirm that this giant rodent cannot really throw its quills. It must make contact. Fortunately, we had the stick between us. © Cynthia Baldauf

Hide and seek with a twig

A rare glimpse of a nine-banded, long-nosed armadillo in broad daylight near its hideout in Big Sandy, Texas. © Marlene Bell

Masked acorn bandit

This young raccoon is eating a live oak acorn shortly after a Texas rain.
© Marlene Bell

The sheepherder

Jose Garzia herds sheep in the mountains of southeastern Colorado. The rancher brings supplies every two weeks to his little camper. He lives with four dogs and two mules, which help move camp and the flock to fresh grazing ground. © Connie Thompson

"Sheepherding sure is lonesome. The mules and dogs do not talk much."

Jose Garzia

Bilko

By Bill Jones

Sergeant Bilko, a fifteen-year-old stout dude-string gelding at a guest ranch in Wyoming, is a schemer, scammer and talented con artist—much like his namesake on the old television series. There is no four-footed animal smarter than a dude horse that has packed around wannabe cowboys for the last ten years or so.

Bilko, more often than not, fails to report during the morning roundups and subsequently makes the AWOL list at least a couple of times a week. Since he also knows all the best hiding places he is often successful in taking several new "recruits" along with him. Adept at opening any and all gates, he occasionally takes a few days off to visit his horse buddies residing at neighboring ranches. If Bilko was a human "teenager," no doubt he would be declared incorrigible in any court of law. The outfit's wranglers, a somewhat cynical bunch, all want to send Bilko on an expense-paid tour of France—in a can.

Bilko can best be described as a black/brown, sorrel/bay and dapple-grey mix. (Never argue politics, religion *or* the color of a horse.) Along with his many talents, Bilko has excellent ears and can hear the door of the grain bin opening from several miles away. He can expertly evaluate a dude's riding ability (or lack thereof) before a foot is even in the stirrup.

Like most fifteen-year-olds, he will invariably try to get away with…well, whatever he can as he takes the path of least resistance. Every month or so one of the wranglers, disgusted with his adolescent antics, will ride him for the day to "tune him up." Bilko always seems to ascertain that this is a prelude to a vacation in Europe and performs like a champion in a national reining competition.

"You know," the wrangler will say afterwards, "this is a pretty good ol' horse. Maybe we should keep him." And he is a pretty good horse—at least for that particular day. Bilko, the consummate fraudster, has once again flimflammed his way out of becoming French cuisine. It works each and every time.

This particular dude outfit entertains guests from strange and exotic places all over the globe. Japan. Great Britain. Israel. Brooklyn. One day, a young couple checks in from the People's Republic of San Francisco. The young woman does not ride and spends her time sketching ranch scenes and skipping after butterflies in the horse pasture. Since their last name contains every letter in the alphabet (sometimes twice), the wranglers, not especially known for their originality, nickname them the Alphabet Couple. Walking by their cabin at night it smells like someone inside is burning skunk weed.

The male half of this couple is a huge, big-bellied guy who wears a little golf hat and a patch over one eye. The wranglers immediately christen him "The Polish Pirate"—not to his face of course.

There is some spirited discussion of this moniker because some maintain a real Polish pirate wears a patch over both eyes. Since dudes (how can I say this politically correctly?) who are "weight challenged" are assigned appropriate load-bearing mounts, the Polish Pirate's horse for the week is…Bilko.

On that first morning, while helping saddle the string, I notice the Polish Pirate whispering in Bilko's ear. Bilko eyes him warily as both ears twitch back and forth like two independent metronomes. The Polish Pirate explains he is just trying to determine Bilko's "life force." I patiently explain that I

Yuk yuk. That was a good one.
© Linda Dufurrena

don't know how things are done in San Francisco, but here in Wyoming we have laws against such weirdness.

One day, I lead a trail ride with Bilko and the Polish Pirate. Bilko, as usual, is lagging about eight thousand yards behind. If he had been walking any slower he would be going backwards. I ride back to check out the problem. Bilko has just stopped for a leisurely little grass snack along the side of the trail. His passenger seems blissfully unconcerned.

"Mr. Lipschitz," I say (names have been changed to protect the lamebrained), "you are going to have to get after Bilko a little bit. I am afraid he will go to sleep while walking, fall and hurt someone. Namely you." I then draw back with an attention-getting little leather quirt I sometimes carry to smack Bilko on the butt.

"*You will not abuse this animal in my presence!*" This is a forceful and direct order from the Polish Pirate. I abruptly cancel the quirt activity. Bilko gives me a smug and insolent look.

I think I see him smiling.

Showing the porker

After months of work and a lot of effort and competition, Sierra Waters from the Willow Springs 4-H Club auctions her prize reserve champion pig in the ring at the Amador County Fair in Plymouth, California. © Larry Angier

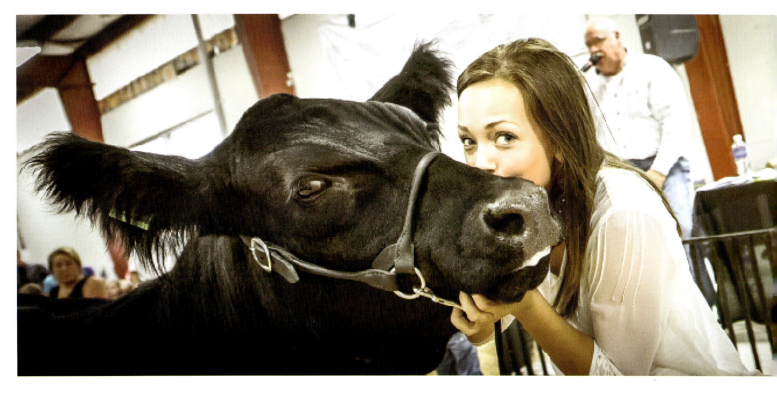

Confidence
Becky Berger of Post Falls, Idaho, is all smiles in the sale ring at the North Idaho Fair with her prizewinning steer. © Chris Holloway

White rabbits
A 4-H girl sells her champion meat rabbits at the junior livestock auction at the Amador County Fair. © Larry Angier

Chicken rustler
Mattley Dell'Orto catches a gray speckled hen at Cuneo Ranch, Jackson, California. © Robin Dell'Orto

Ferruginous hawk
A fitting raptor for wide skies and windswept plains of the West, and with a wingspan up to sixty inches, its prey includes ground squirrels, snakes, young jackrabbits and anything else it can get its claws on. The females are larger than the males. © Larry Turner

"On motionless wing they emerge from the lifting mists, sweep a final arc of sky, and settle in clangorous descending spirals to their feeding grounds. A new day has begun on the crane marsh."

Aldo Leopold, "Sand County Almanac," 1949

Sandhill cranes
Mates take to the sky above Surprise Valley, California.
© Larry Turner

Cowboys in yellow slickers

These McGarva Ranch cowboys are entering the Blue Lake allotment located in the Warner Mountains of eastern California. Blue Lake sits in a pine and fir forest on the Modoc-Lassen county line and this range was owned by the McGarva family until the Forest Service bought it in 1939. A good stream runs through the meadows which makes it ideal for the cattle from midsummer until October. These cowboys are about to bring the cattle down from the high country to their winter feedground in Likely, California. That morning's snow was not expected, or they would have saddled up the day before. © Duane McGarva

Calving in a blizzard

Ken Clark checks heavies to see if they need help with calving in Smoot, Wyoming. © Skye Clark

A sea of green

Cowboys round up a herd of Black Angus and Charolais cattle on a ranch near Cleveland, Montana.
© Todd Klassy

I hope my calf is small

Lane Buzzetti, age four, works out his loop at the Buzzetti family ranch in Lamoille, Nevada.
© Jessica Brandi Lifland

Catching the loop

Hunewill Ranch, Bridgeport, California.
© Terri Butler

Del viento

T.J. Horton throws a fancy hip shot to catch the calf's back legs during spring branding at the Grindstone Ranch in Wyoming. Cole Butner is the header.
© Skye Clark

"Wanton killers as the coyotes are, one bobcat can often work greater destruction in a single night, for it comes softly on the flock, does not scatter it, kills quickly without alarm, and since cats take little besides the blood and soft parts of the throat, one requires a good bunch of lambs for a meal."

Mary Austin, "The Flock," 1906

Two cute
Bum lambs are nurtured at the home ranch.
© Linda Dufurrena

Bobcat family

Windy Hill, Washoe County, Nevada.
© Diane McAllister

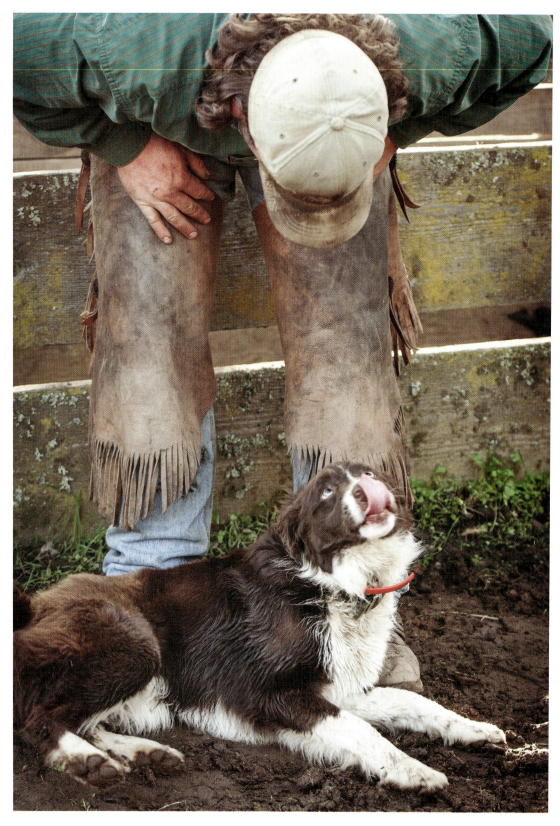

The reprimand

Clinton Brownlie takes a break and talks with his cow dog during winter branding with the Dell'Orto family in Amador County, California. © Larry Angier

Mexican ground squirrel

© Scott Linstead/Tom Stack & Associates

Ground squirrels
By Carolyn Dufurrena

They may be cute, but they demolish the fields, digging tunnels, eating the roots of the alfalfa. They get so thick sometimes you lose the whole field. They're cannibalistic, too. You'll see one dead on the highway, the Idaho cowboy said, and thirty minutes later, there are four more of them there, cleaning up the remains.

    Ah, yes, the circle of life, said his girlfriend. The pancake of life.

Rock squirrel

© Terrence Ross/Tom Stack & Associates

"It is notable that the best sheepdogs are most like wolves in habit, the erect triangular ears, the long thin muzzle, the sag of the bushy tail, the thick mane-like hackles."

Mary Austin, "The Flock," 1906

Part of the crew

This dog keeps an eye on the cowboys' gear loaded on the wagon during the Padlock Ranch branding in Dayton, Wyoming.
© Guy de Galard

Riding the team

Lou Roberts brings the workhorses home from the feed ground in Daniel, Wyoming. © Jennifer Roberts

Forty field hands for the noon meal

By Carolyn Dufurrena

Well into his seventies, the old man was still governed by the austerity of his youth. Never a string thrown away but rewound onto the roll in the pantry. Employees could come and use the old black dial-up phone in that pantry, there would be no more phone lines added across the field.

Asparagus planted decades earlier along an orchard-grass-choked ditch was still harvested, though it was thick and rank and could have done with transplanting to a less hostile neighborhood. There was no softness in him, at first glance, and even second. He had lived his life surrounded by the rugged landscape and the endless sky, and by the animals that lived in that landscape. Still, there was the day he was showing the new cowboy around the place, pointing with his chin and growling along about feed on the mountain and the BLM.

Suddenly he slammed on the brakes, nearly throwing the kid into the windshield. "Look!" he exclaimed. "Baby ducks!" Just like the policeman in the Robert McCloskey tale of ducklings on the Boston Commons, he let the dust settle in the road as the mallard hen and her brood made their way across the gravel.

One afternoon not long after, a badger bolted across the road from the alfalfa field into his machine shop. Two Mexican field hands were hot after it, shovels in hand, until he stopped them. "Leave her be, she'll keep the varmints down."

When the weather got really hot, mid-July suffocating, his wife made a habit of leaving the pantry door into the garden open. A six-foot-long bullsnake moved in and made its home under the refrigerator, where it could stay cool on the concrete floor, emerging at twilight to scour the garden for mice and what-have-you. Visitors who needed to make a phone call in that pantry regularly discovered what appeared to be a slow-moving coiled rope as it withdrew beneath the appliance. The old woman was shocked to discover that most folks thought that behavior odd.

There were the two baby ravens, which some miner types brought into the ranch headquarters from the old CCC camp down the road, where a

Mallard drake
© Diane McAllister

lone chimney still stood. Ravens had nested in the chimney for decades, and the men, who came into the headquarters to use the pay phone, thought it would be a good trade, a moment of humor.

"They were miserable sonsabitches," the ranch

Bullsnake
A nonvenomous constrictor, adults average from four to six feet.
© Larry Turner

manager said. "Hopped into the pickup trucks when the men were eating lunch," forty field hands in for the noontime meal. "They'd steal the keys out of the vehicles and stash them somewhere," stole everything shiny in fact, and pecked at the toddlers' heads while their mothers were busy in the gardens. Still, they survived for an inordinately long time, in and out of truck cabs and cars that had left their windows down in summer's heat, in and out of the shops foraging for bolts and wing nuts.

Out in the country, animals of all kinds invade our boundaries, or perhaps our boundaries are softened to include them among our familiars. They are not pets: most are nowhere near tame, but there's an agreed-upon symbiosis that comes from occupying the same space.

Raven
A thief and an opportunist.
© Mark Hayward

"The hawk follows the badger, the coyote the carrion crow, and from their aerial station the buzzards watch each other."

Mary Austin, "The Flock," 1906

Drying my wings
One of many turkey vultures perches on a pile of rocks in early morning in the Bilk Creek Mountains of northern Nevada. © Larry Angier

Yellow songster
A western meadowlark in the springtime on a ranch outside Merrill, Oregon. This is Oregon's state bird. © Larry Turner

Spring migration
Pintail ducks in the Lower Klamath National Wildlife Refuge. All migratory birds feed on the refuge, and feast on irrigated pasture and crop stubble on local farms and ranches. © Larry Turner

Perpetual battle
Wild stallions at a water hole outside of Fernley, Nevada, fight for which mares will drink first. © Sandy Tibbals

Mustangs
By Tim Findley

For the (wild) horses we have today, you have to blame Columbus, who on his second voyage brought horses as well as other livestock to Hispaniola. After that, the colony-seeking king of Spain directed that every expedition to the New World would carry horses.

Horses in the arid and sparsely populated Silver State were made abundant for the first time when desperate emigrants turned their horses loose, or, as often, ate them. The population of unclaimed horses grew so great that at one point in the 1870s the state of Nevada put a bounty on them.

Today, mustangs have become a collective albatross on federal Interior policy that satisfies nobody.

Cool water

J Spear ranch horses take a sunset drink outside Paisley, Oregon.
© Larry Turner

Winter's majestic elk
Jackson Hole, Wyoming.
© Sarah E. Wagoner

Gentle strength

Eighteen-year-old Eric Nelson holds three border collies.
© Robin L. Green

Can I have some?

One plate, three mouths. Stan Dell'Orto isn't ready to share the delicious lunch prepared by Pati Wooster at the Wooster family's branding at the Henry Ranch in Copperopolis, California.
© Robin Dell'Orto

Ridin' shotgun
Ted Harris and dog Shep, Whitehorse Ranch, Oregon. © Larry Turner

"**Dogs feel very strongly that they should always go with you in the car, in case the need should arise for them to bark violently at nothing, right in your ear.**"

Dave Barry, Pulitzer prize-winning author and columnist

Boy's keeper
Jordan Gravette and his dog Slick at the Dell'Orto/Mattley Ranch in Jackson, California. © Robin Dell'Orto

> **"The owls lived in the shop in the summertime, and they'd hoot at each other across the big echoing space. They sounded like kids, hollering down the canyon."**
>
> Tim Dufurrena, rancher

Ground-loving flyers
Valley quail, handsome and rough, fly on short, broad wings but spend most of their lives on the ground. Malin, Oregon.
© Larry Turner

Great horned owl

By Rene Maestrejuan

The wink
Great horned owl flashes a feather-covered eyelid.
© Tom & Therisa Stack/Tom Stack & Associates

Great horned owls nested in the poplar trees around the ranch headquarters. As they grew and learned to fly, they tried to perch on nearby power poles. Their adult wingspan might reach almost five feet, and inevitably their wings would touch the wires as they landed on the crossbars. The electric shock would knock them to the ground and sometimes paralyze them temporarily. If they survived, I'd bring them into the yard to try to save them.

Sometimes they'd perch on the fence in the rain, wings spread, fluffing their feathers as if taking a shower. A raptor scientist developed an L-shaped bar that prevented them from landing on the crossbars and electrocuting themselves. I convinced the local power company to install a few of these devices near the poplars so more owls would survive.

We left the ranch. In the years following, workers who had moved there, believing the owls were messengers of death, shot them all.

First flight surprise
© Sheree Jensen

Grain!
Saddle horses share a feed bin at a ranch near LaGrange, Wyoming.
© Bruce Most

Are you ready?
My husband's mare, Baby, peers in the window hoping for a treat. Her favorite is peanut butter dog biscuits. Andy claimed her name was embarrassing for a cowboy horse but figured it was better than using her real name, "Honey Stop the Show." The Daniels Ranch, Wisdom, Montana. © Cynthia Baldauf

Heavy horses

Clark Jensen with a few of his shires in Nebraska. Tina, a three-year-old filly, held the record for tallest horse in the world at twenty hands barefoot. © Ozana Sturgeon

Elk mother and baby
Off-camera, a grizzly approaches this cow elk, who gathers up her fawn in Yellowstone Park, Wyoming.
© Diane McAllister

"Nourishing is in fact the greater part of mothering."

Mary Austin, "The Flock," 1906

Sleeping coyote pups
Arrow Creek, Washoe County, Nevada. © Diane McAllister

Hummingbird
Sharing the meal.
© Diane McAllister

> "A dog may be man's best friend but the horse wrote history."
>
> Unknown

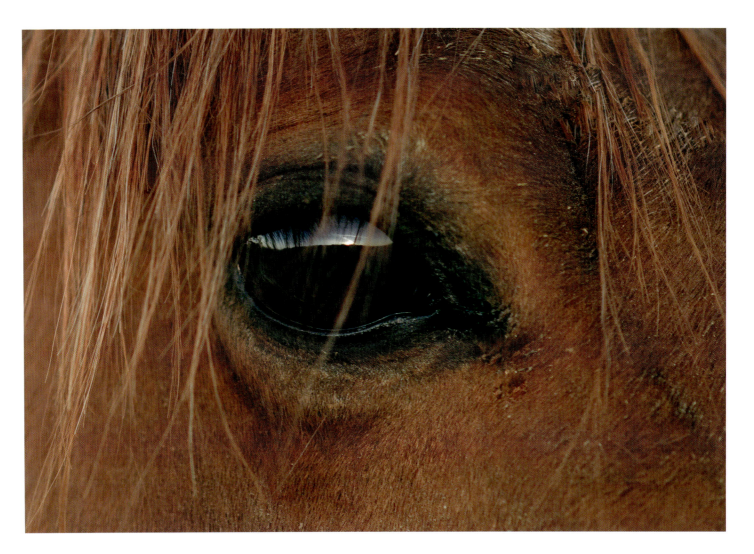

Sunset in his eye
© Linda Dufurrena

Snow at the barn
© Ozana Sturgeon

Pinkey was too much help

Reed Clark gets his dog Pinkey out of the roping trap as the family gets ready to vaccinate fall calves for the Grindstone Ranch in Daniel, Wyoming. © Skye Clark

Little Edie can get them moving
Gathering steers for the Valente family roundup in Eugene, California. © Robin Dell'Orto

A truly durable joke
By Vess Quinlan

When we had been on our run-down formerly bank-owned outfit for a month or so, our newly hired man, Leo, brought a relative to visit.

"Boss, I want you to meet my uncle Placido. He works for the government," Leo said proudly.

Placido was the smallest of Leo's many uncles and the most wrinkled. He ranked near the top of the uncle age range and though nearly eighty years old continued to work as if he were thirty. One could never be quite sure if his busy brown eyes revealed a natural good humor or a penchant for pranks and mischief. He resembled an amused brown elf bent slightly forward by years of manual labor.

After a bit of polite conversation, he got down to business and made his pitch with the distinctive accent, wonderful word choice, and delightful phrasing of those who, while comfortable with English, really prefer to speak Spanish.

Mr. Gardunio drew an official-looking document from his pocket and said: "Mr. Quinlan, I have been noticing that those prairie dogs are getting pretty bad in that little horse pasture across from your alfalfa. If you will sign this paper, I will cure those prairie dogs."

The document was in two parts from the state agency in charge of predator and pest control. One part required a legal description and granted permission. The other part had a blank for the number of acres to be treated and authorized payment from a tax levied against livestock growers and farmers. The complete legal description and number of acres to be treated had been filled in neatly and correctly.

I suspected that Placido Gardunio had augmented his income from a small farm by curing the prairie dogs every now and then.

"You must sign both places," the old man said, "or the state will not pay me."

I signed both places and said: "Mr. Gardunio, I will be pleased to have you cure my prairie dogs. But if I were you, I would not cure them too hard. I would always leave a few so there will be money next year."

The old man smiled and said: "Leo, I think I will like your new boss. That was a pretty good joke for a gringo. And it is true too."

I guess it was a pretty good joke because it became ritual and every year, along in May, for nearly twenty years, the little man would knock softly on my door, sip his coffee, and make his pitch. We repeated the durable little joke almost word for word until Placido, true to his name, died quietly in his sleep one cold January night.

If prairie dogs knew about holidays they would have declared one at the passing of Placido Gardunio, because never again would they cower in their cozy homes in the ground while the bent shadow of their number-one enemy moved slowly from mound to mound with his little tin scoop and pail of poison pellets.

The prairie dog town prospers, post Placido. The state never replaced him or any other predator and pest control contractor. The agency decided to threaten pests and predators from an office in downtown Denver.

Fortunately for my alfalfa, owls patrolling the county road at night and a pair of golden eagles perched atop the power poles by day force expansion of the prairie dog town westward into the pasture and away from the alfalfa field.

Only brave or foolhardy prairie dogs will risk scampering past the owls at night to gorge on my alfalfa. And when the foolish ones waddle back at daylight, their furry bellies stuffed with the forbidden legume, they make easy picking for the eagles.

I will eventually have to do something about the prolific little devils because they use up land like crazed real estate developers. But I fear that should I travel to Denver and wander the halls of state government, I might see a door with the words "Office of Pest and Predator Control" sten-

Only brave or foolhardy prairie dogs will risk scampering past the owls at night to gorge on my alfalfa. And when the foolish ones waddle back at daylight, their furry bellies stuffed with the forbidden legume, they make easy picking for the eagles.

Prairie dog
Enjoying Utah sunshine.
© Carol Lister

ciled on the opaque glass. I might find a fresh-faced young person with a degree in wildlife biology, or some such thing, who would never dream of knocking on anyone's door and shyly offering to cure their prairie dogs.

This young person might leave off shuffling important papers to hear my complaint and decide to use the rare opportunity of meeting an actual taxpayer to brag about agency efficiency and explain some powerful new technology to control pests and predators.

"Mr. Quinlan," this person might say, "if you fill out these papers, and sign all sixteen places, those prairie dogs don't have a chance."

I shall not travel to Denver and seek out the humorless person I have imagined. I am afraid the bureaucrat might not understand "The durable little joke" and cure my prairie dogs too hard.

The owls and eagles would starve out and move on. I would miss them and miss the excited barks of the silly little prairie dogs. Just as every year, along in May, I miss the soft knock of Placido Gardunio.

Riding the mist
Gathering cattle to brand calves near Clements, California.
© Debbie Bell

Boss cat

This monster known as Fisher Cat is a Maine Coon. He lives at the horse barn and does his best to serve as greeter. In his free time he keeps the rodent population at bay. The Williams Ranch, Wisdom, Montana. © Cynthia Baldauf

Morning scratch

Elaine Davies says hello to her sow Sally at Roaring Springs Ranch. Elaine's husband, Stacy, manages this large spread on the high desert based in Frenchglen, Oregon.
© Larry Turner

"People and animals are supposed to be together. We spent quite a lot of time evolving together, and we used to be partners. Now people are cut off from animals unless they have a dog or a cat."

Temple Grandin, "Animals in Translation," 2006

Where's Mom?
After heavy rain and lots of mud, this calf found a dry place to nap—in the feed rack! McGarva Ranch, Likely, California. © Duane McGarva

Ducks
Northern shovelers rise from the water at Tule Lake National Wildlife Refuge, California. © Larry Turner

Whoops! I forgot to pray
Cooper's hawk.
© Diane McAllister

Decades of protection
By James Ployhar

In 1918, people were killing migratory birds for their plumage. We passed the Migratory Bird Treaty Act because some species of migratory waterfowl were endangered. Fifty-five years later, in 1973, we passed the Endangered Species Act to protect all endangered birds and animals. These acts were amended numerous times in the years that followed. All predatory birds were added, although some are not endangered and some are not migratory. Last year, Helena's Last Chance Audubon Society counted 2,630 golden eagles migrating through the Big Belt Mountains. Many of these winter here in central Montana. How many grouse and pheasants does it take to feed 2,600 eagles each day?

After forty-three years of protection, the country is full of raptors and the grouse are endangered. Society controls predatory people, predatory animals, and predatory plants. Why not predatory birds?

Water dance
A glossy-faced ibis, one of the species protected under the Migratory Bird Treaty Act, does a little water dance in a flooded farm field outside Tulelake, California. © Larry Turner

Neighboring
Millions of birds in the Lower Klamath National Wildlife Refuge: swans, ducks and geese on ice and open water at Lower Klamath National Wildlife Refuge, California.
© Larry Turner

"[A] migrating goose, staking two hundred miles of black night on the chance of finding a hole in the lake, has no easy chance for retreat. His arrival carries the conviction of a prophet who has burned his bridges."

Aldo Leopold, "Sand County Almanac," 1949

Last day of the season, Big Hole Valley, Montana

The Harold Peterson crew poses on a buck rake. They are one of the last families in the valley still stacking loose hay using a beaverslide. Originally called the Beaverhead County Slide Stacker, the machine was invented in 1908 by two Big Hole ranchers and is still in use today. The only change in the last hundred years is the addition of engines for the rakes and hoists. Each summer the Peterson crew is made up entirely of family—some of whom use their entire vacation to come for the annual ritual. © Cynthia Baldauf

Steering with my boots

Harold Peterson's grandson, Malcolm, carefully watches his grandpa finish cleaning the leftover hay from around the twenty-ton stack. The instant Harold rounds the corner headed for the new stack yard, Malcolm takes liberties with his driving.
© Cynthia Baldauf

Winter feeding

The Heidi Hirschy family still feeds with work horses, more reliable than tractors during the long frigid winters. Dan Hosko, at the lines, drives three wide on the PO Ranch. © Cynthia Baldauf

Topping off the stack

Dean Peterson rides the basket to the top of the beaverslide with a pitchfork. He builds a smooth, rounded crown on the thirty-foot stack, which forms a watershield, ensuring that the hay inside stays fresh. Some stacks opened after ten years are still bright green on the inside. © Cynthia Baldauf

Love the ears

Grass Valley, California.
© Jurij Strutynsky

Suspicion
Callie the barn cat gets annoyed at a curious colt.
Cedar Creek Ranch, Dillon, Montana. © Susan Marxer

Go girls!
It's a snowy day moving cattle to spring permit ground. Alder Creek Ranch, north-central Nevada.
© Janet Johnson

Working up a sweat

Cowboy Jay Hoggan spends winters feeding a thousand elk in the Gros Ventre Range in Wyoming. He also trains the teams. This pair—a seasoned veteran and a novice—had just long-trotted five miles from his rustic Forest Service cabin to load up at the Alkali feed ground. © Pam White

Frozen

Weanlings in a corral on a frosty morning in central Wyoming.
© Jennifer DeFreece

The rooster
© Linda Dufurrena

The raven

By John Dufurrena

We raised the raven in the big chicken coop at the ranch till it could fly. He never did leave the ranch headquarters, flew back and forth wherever he felt like. He was so smart, he could hear the cook come out of the cookhouse after cleaning up. He'd be out in the shop and hear the door close, and make a beeline for the scraps the cook was leaving out for the cats. He'd fly right back and beat 'em off.

He could smell fear on us kids. If one of the littler ones was scared of him, he'd peck and pester that kid mercilessly. My little brother Joe was still in diapers, and he was terrified of that raven that would peck at his diaper and flap in his face.

He liked me, though, because I wasn't scared of him. He'd perch on my shoulder and walk around with me.

He did love anything shiny. We had a couple of hay contractors that summer, sleeping in an Army pup tent out behind the bunkhouse. That black bird would get into their tent and steal their stuff. They hated him. We had him for a couple of years, and I think maybe at the end a bobcat killed him. But it could have been somebody shot him finally for being so annoying.

Juvenile raven begs for food
Carson City, Nevada.
© Valerie Dutter

Nevada mustangs
Mustangs are domesticated herd animals gone feral. They require huge amounts of feed and water which do not exist in much of their present habitat in the Great Basin. They lack the natural ability to control herd populations at sustainable levels and must be managed extensively. The herd doubles every four or five years. © Alan Hart

> **"Feral horses run free and seem to enjoy it. Even when life gets tough, it's best to follow the wind. Or is it? An independent creature will take the bit and saddle for life. But does it long for some tenuous freedom? Or be satisfied with a ration of oats?"**
>
> John Bardwell

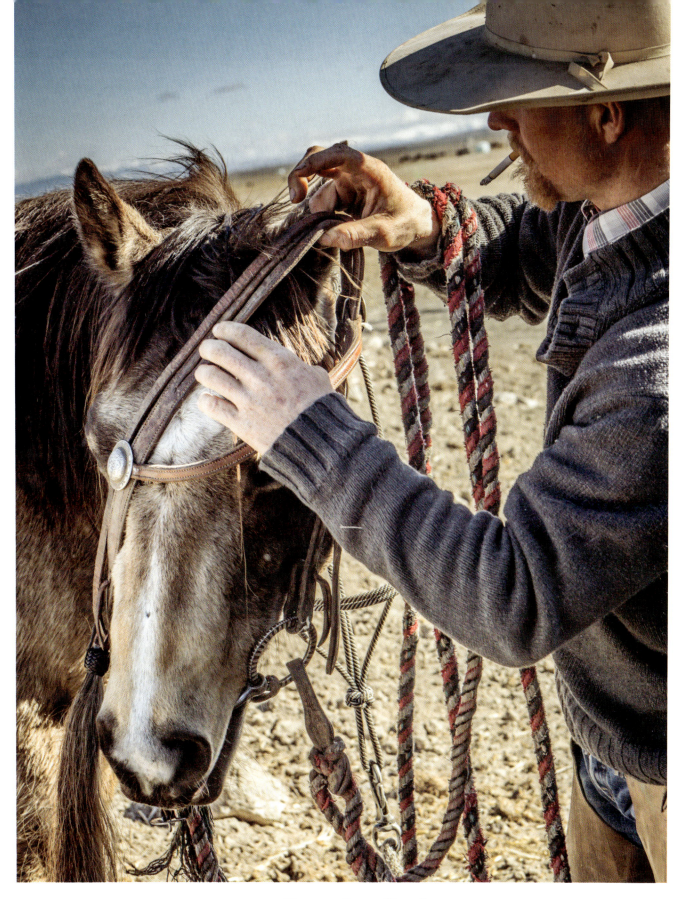

Dressing the horse

Gabe Clark bridles his colt to brand calves at a ranch in Grays Lake, Idaho.
© Skye Clark

After lunch
Grizzly mom and cub. © Eberhard Brunner

"The grizzly disappeared from California in 1922, hundreds of years after the coming of sheep and shepherds, but not long after the coming of summer campers."

Barney Nelson, "The Wild and the Domestic," 2000

Elk pride
© Mark Hayward

Ready to face the world
Twin mule deer fawns. © Gerri Duke

"**Orphaned fawns and antelope kids grow up in the yards, bottle fed till they're old enough to manage on their own. One neighbor even had a bobcat kitten that perched up high on the rock mantel of his fireplace, still as death, as a statue. A visitor admired the mount, assuming the kit was stuffed—until it blinked its yellow eyes and jumped away.**"

Carolyn Dufurrena

New legs

A newborn calf stands up for the first time on the D2 Ranch in North Powder, Oregon.
© Sarah B. Anderson

Hello, babies!
Daphne Fiona greets her friends in the corral at the Schatz Ranch outside Otto, Wyoming.
© Marion Dickinson

Feeding the black lamb
Grace McGarva takes her turn feeding the leppy lambs at her grandparents' ranch in Choteau, Montana. © Cynthia Baldauf

Science lesson, Dog River school

By Carolyn Dufurrena

The first expedition to the pond at Five Mile was no more than a bumpy short drive into the foothills, courtesy of a few parents with Suburbans and Jeeps. The children were armed with plastic pitchers, bowls, spoons, and the invitation to collect anything that seemed worth further scrutiny.

Jacqueline stood transfixed, staring at the water. Dark hair rippled down her back. She was small for a seven-year-old, half Mexican, half black, her beautiful great brown eyes full of intelligence and more pain than a seven-year-old should know. She held a two-quart pitcher against skinny pink tights, waiting for permission, and then not waiting.

The children spread out around the shallow pond and along the stream that ran down to the trough below, poking at hummocks, turning over rocks, gathering treasures. Soon Jacqueline was up to her knees in water rich with algae and creatures, spooning green moss and squirming invertebrates into her jug, to be dumped into a five-gallon bucket for the lesson.

Back in the little school, concrete walls cool in the spring afternoon, the long white plastic table became their laboratory, presided over by the white-bearded scientist in his soft sheepskin moccasins. Jacqueline had her tiny monster captured

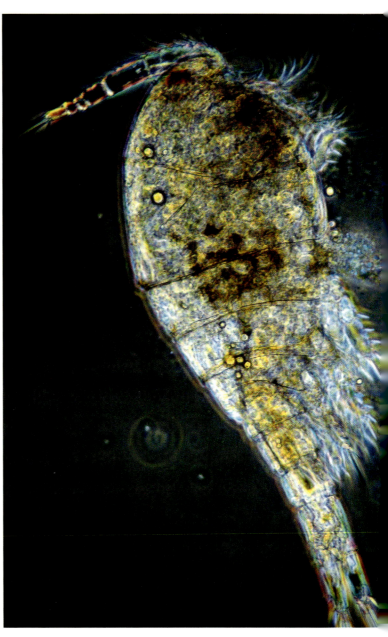

Cyclops, freshwater crustacean
© Tom Stack/Tom Stack & Associates

in a tablespoon ladled out onto the white expanse.

"Ah," he said, his brown eyes crinkling. *"Daphnia."*

She stood carefully, watching it swim around its tiny pond. A small miracle of technology, a slide projector and a deep-well slide allowed live creatures to be examined. She poured her creature into the slide, closed the cover. It slid before the projector's lamp, and in a moment the shape, as large as the full moon, brought everyone to a silent standstill.

The monster, *Daphnia*, swam around the white circle on the wall. Fully three feet across, its huge, hairy appendages waving, working its claws. It was eating the moon. Not even the old man had a word to say.

Salt Grass Meadow, Coyote Creek

The white-bearded old man kept a sharp eye as they crept up the rocky canyon, children wedged into the pickup truck. He saw the flooded saltgrass meadow for what it was.

"Get out, get out!" he exclaimed. "We must investigate."

Salt grass is short, coarse, spiky, and uncomfortable to walk through. The creek had overflowed its banks, flooding the small streamside meadow with two inches of swiftly running water. The grass was alive with tadpoles, thousands of them, an inch long, struggling through the sharp blades with the current. The children harvested them by the handful, capturing them in buckets and jars and plastic bags.

Moss and watercress clung to the banks of the stream. The children heaved and scraped at a heavy basalt boulder, trying to roll it, to discover what lay beneath. One hairy ten-legged creature, tiny in its ferocity, clung to the underside of the rock. Christened Toebiter, it found itself out of the swift flow of the stream and into a Mason jar with the tadpoles and one long thread-thin red worm. It clamped on to a stick, glaring at the world outside. But as dominating as the tiny arthropod appeared in the fast water of the creek, it was helpless in still water. Overnight the threadlike red worm attached itself to Toebiter's temple, carapace split open all along his back, and he was dead by morning, his body slowly consumed by snails.

Chow time!
Running for the hay truck at the Twin Mountain Ranch near Guernsey, Wyoming. © Millie Roesch

Born in a blizzard
Ken Clark takes a newborn calf to the barn to warm up. Mama cow won't let him out of her sight.
© Skye Clark

Brrrrrr

Frosted mama

Black heifer in a spring blizzard at the Clark Ranch in Smoot, Wyoming.
© Skye Clark

It's warmer in the trees
McGarva cattle are being moved from summer range on October 15—one day too late! Warner Mountains, California.
© Duane McGarva

One cold day

Never too chilly to work
Clinton Pankratz works through a driving snow on the Kellam Ranch near Cleveland, Montana. © Todd Klassy

Looking for cover
Twin Mountain Ranch, Guernsey, Wyoming.
© Millie Roesch

Tending the woollies

One in a hundred
Sheep from Lost River Land and Livestock head for the high country in the Caribou-Targhee National Forest in Idaho. © Cindy Quigley

Professional shearers
Harold Miller Ranch, Worland, Wyoming. © Marion Dickinson

Bellowing
American bison. © Pamela S. Wickkiser

Looking for a fight or a date?

Tracking this bull moose along the Big Hole near Fishtrap, Montana, was a lifetime thrill. He was almost black with a gleaming coat. I could hear him grunt and call and the water as it dribbled from his mouth. Fortunately, he paid me no attention. My hands shook and my heart beat so loudly I was shocked he couldn't hear it. Afterward, I said a prayer of thanks and smiled for a week. © Cynthia Baldauf

Bison eye
© Pamela S. Wickkiser

Whirlaway: A shot of used grass

By Linda M. Hasselstrom

We'd named the old black whiteface cow for a famous racehorse, because she was fast on the straightaway and tricky on the curves. Besides speed, Whirlaway possessed intelligence, or instinct if you prefer, that alerted her when humans were going to do something she wouldn't like. She preferred not to cooperate with them.

Whenever we moved the cattle anywhere, she ran the opposite direction. If she had a calf, it galloped along in her wake, eyeballs rolling white, tail straight in the air just like Mama's, genetically programmed to cause trouble.

We knew she'd be difficult to handle when we gathered cows that fall, culling out the old ones for sale. We'd already discussed the alternatives: it was time to sell her because she was fifteen years old, and dry. That is, she was not carrying a calf, so she would not contribute the next year to the crop we rely on to pay the bills. Had she been younger, we'd have kept her, giving her a year's vacation and relying on her good breeding to pay us back in better health and future calves. But at fifteen, she was nearly at the end of her productive life. We can't afford to run a nursing home for elderly cows, feeding them while they stand around the pasture waiting to die. Best to sell her this fall, rather than risk her teeth going bad during the coming winter, causing her to starve and suffer.

Furthermore, she was pastured three miles from the corrals, the only place where we had plank fences tall and strong enough to guide her into a truck to haul her away. My father, having spent fifteen years handling the cow quietly in the hope she'd calm down, suggested half in jest that we just shoot her in the pasture and consider it our donation to the coyotes and vultures. "Might be the most sensible thing we could do," he pointed out. "Because she's going to tear down fences and run you around, and we'll be lucky if you or the horse doesn't break a leg before we get her outta there."

Foolishly optimistic, I convinced my husband, George, that I could drive her to the corrals with the rest of the cattle we planned to sell. I eased the horse along behind the little bunch of cattle, paying no attention to Whirlaway. If all the other cattle moved ahead of the horse, maybe she'd follow them out the gate and down the trail home.

My horse that day was Oliver, a beautiful gray part-Arab with a wonderfully easy gait. But he was lazy, willing to get along with as little work as possible. Only when he was really angry, hot, and tired did he turn into the cutting horse his sainted mother was. Then he spun and pivoted on his hind feet, slashing back and forth behind a cow, anticipating every move she made, crowding her with his chest, biting when he could, until she had no choice but to go in the direction we chose. Whenever you see a "cowboy" yelling and swinging his rope as he thunders along behind a herd of cows, he's either in a movie, or he doesn't own the cows and he may soon be unemployed. In real life, running cattle causes them to lose hundreds of pounds on a hot day, weight which translates into hard-earned money lost because of haste or ignorance.

When I'm handling cattle, I don't care if my horse is fast, but it must be nimble and alert, be smart enough to anticipate a cow's moves and turn with her to block her escape before she breaks into a run.

The rest of the cattle were quiet as they reached the gate George had opened. Ostentatiously relaxed

The troublemaker
A tough South Dakota cow. © Larry Angier

for Whirlaway's benefit, he leaned against the pickup nearby with his son, Mike, a summer visitor. I'd slowed the horse so much a few cows began stopping every few steps to graze. Quietly, I maneuvered among them, gently separating the ones to be sold. Each time one or more ambled into a direct line with the gate, I'd speak to the horse, maybe trot a little as I eased them through.

Finally, every cow we wanted to sell was outside the gate. Except Whirlaway. While the others grazed quietly, she stood beside the fence, head up, ears erect, snorting.

I turned the horse and ambled her way. She threw her head higher, raised her tail, and trotted around me to join the cows we planned to leave in the pasture. I reconsidered, then gathered the whole bunch and aimed them all at the gate, waving at George. He nodded and drove the pickup

127

away through the gate, encouraging the cows already cut out for sale to move on down the road. If Whirlaway followed the second bunch quietly through the gate, putting the rest of them back into the pasture would still be less trouble than we usually had cutting her out of a crowd.

Nope. The other cows trotted between the posts in a neat line. When Whirlaway was four steps from the gate with me close behind her, she turned inside out and vanished. I spun the horse and whipped around her again. Again she ducked aside at the last instant.

The third time we got close to the gate, Oliver shoved Whirlaway with his shoulder while I yelled and hit her with the reins. She raised her tail and shot out a stream of used grass, splashing green chunks all over his chest and side, over my leg and the saddle.

Annoyed, Oliver opened his mouth to bite the cow on the hip. She raised her tail. He reconsidered, snapping his mouth shut so hard his teeth clattered. The cow ran off. I eased one foot out of the stirrup to rest a moment. George drove back, shut the gate, and handed me the water jug while I explained method number three: I'd tire the cow into giving up.

Trotting the horse, I simply followed her wherever she went, back and forth on the flat. Fortunately, since I was watching the cow and the horse's ears so I could lean with quick turns instead of falling out of the saddle, prairie dogs have not invaded this spot. Each time the cow got close to the gate, George and Mike would move out from the opening so she'd have a clear view of the rest of the cows grazing outside.

Half an hour of trotting made my horse mad enough to get serious about his job. The tall autumn grass was slick and treacherous. Each time he made a turn so tight his body was nearly horizontal to the ground, I feared he'd fall, but he never even slipped. He trotted closer and closer to her, snapping his teeth.

Then Whirlaway kicked him in the chest. He gasped, snorted, and bit her tail. Unlike horses, cows rarely kick with both hind legs at once, but

Annoyed, Oliver opened his mouth to bite the cow on the hip. She raised her tail. He reconsidered, snapping his mouth shut so hard his teeth clattered.

Whirlaway kicked again just as the horse turned, connecting with my knee with one back hoof, my ankle with the other. The shock was so intense I was absolutely sure the ankle was broken. Then the pain hit and I reined the horse in, mumbling that I'd have to let the damn cow go so we could get to the damn hospital before the damn ankle swelled so much they had to cut the damn boot off. Then my whole leg went numb, and I kicked the horse into a gallop to catch up to the cow.

Whirlaway made a wide circle down into a gully and up the side, with Oliver right behind her. When she reached the top, she spun, lowered her head, and roared back down the hill. Her head struck Oliver's chest and lifted his front feet off the ground. I was yelling words I hoped my stepson didn't know as I pictured myself with the horse on top of me, but Oliver slid sideways as the cow hurtled past. I've seen lots of bovine escape maneuvers, but Whirlaway was the only cow who ever tried to tip my horse over.

George, realizing the cow was working us away from the gate, had put the cows we weren't going to sell back into the pasture. Now he shut the gate and came racing toward us in the pickup, Mike bouncing beside him on the seat, trying to get ahead of the cow before she headed into rough ground. Faster, Whirlaway ran straight down a ten-foot bluff. George veered off with the pickup, but the horse and I slid down in an avalanche of rocks. By the time George caught up, we'd covered nearly a mile and the cow was outrunning the horse. George drove up beside her and forced her to turn. I kept the horse right on her heels while the pickup detoured around another gully.

For a while, we alternated following the cow. Whenever George took a detour, I'd see posts, baling wire, fence stretchers, and all the other essential junk in our pickup hanging suspended in a cloud of dust as the truck ricocheted from rock to rock, billowing black exhaust. Whirlaway kicked the pickup bumper. She swung her head and smashed a door panel. Once, she dashed straight into a tight four-strand barbed-wire fence. The recoil knocked her back on her haunches. The next time she swung her head against the truck door, she smeared blood from a dozen small cuts over the door.

Finally, she trotted down the final slope into the most distant corner of the pasture. Her head swung as she looked at the cross fence and at the other corner of the pasture a half mile away. I mumbled a prayer that she wouldn't jump into the railroad right-of-way, since we have no gates into it, and the mess of old ties and cable left by the railroad crews makes it almost impossible to ride a horse there. She might have tried to climb or jump any of the fences. Instead, without pausing to rest, she turned and began to plod toward the gate, two miles back. Running with sweat, all of us followed her back. Beaten, she never once looked around as we all trudged through the gate.

Later that week, she destroyed several sections of two-by-eight planks six feet high, broke several ropes, and dealt bruises and scrapes to all of us before we got her in the truck, but that's another story. When we finally got her loaded in the truck and headed for the sale barn, she looked fat and healthy. We could see no cuts on her head, no visible evidence of her last epic struggle. My ankle and knee turned purple and green and remained swollen for a couple of weeks.

Whirlaway had to be sold, and we had to get her out of the pasture in order to sell her. If we'd let her get away from us that day, we'd have had the same rodeo another day. Not all range cows are as hard to corral as Whirlaway, but it wasn't especially unusual for us to spend a hard halfday's work getting a wild cow out of the pasture either. Whenever a city friend envies us the ranching life and says, "All you have to do is sit around and watch those cows get fat," I just nod and raise my glass of iced tea in a salute to Whirlaway.

Excerpted from "Between Grass & Sky" published by University of Nevada Press, 2002.

> **"Wildcats, cougars, coyotes and bears are merely incidents of the day's work, like putting on stiff boots in the morning, or running out of garlic."**
>
> Mary Austin, "The Flock," 1906

One big mouthful
Merganser duck with a kokanee salmon at Taylor Lake, California. © Linda Hammond

Sweet salmon
Grizzly near Kodiak Island, Alaska.
© Mark Hayward

Just fishin'

The ultimate digger
Badgers have short legs for burrowing and digging. Their holes in pastures cripple many horses.
© Tom & Therisa Stack/Tom Stack & Associates

Striped skunks
Four or more kits travel along a ditch together. They are so close they are tough to count. © Larry Angier

Who knew coyotes could read?
Whiskey Springs, Nevada. © Patricia Neely

Critters or varmints?
By John Bardwell

Some critters are varmints. Some folks are varmints. Depends on who you ask. Mostly, a critter is like a tomato or a watermelon, where a varmint is like cheatgrass.

Some people think anything with more than two legs is a critter, some more adorable and precious than the next. But if it eats your grain, your livestock, or Fluffy the cat (cats are another matter), then it could be a varmint, or just misunderstood.

Critters can turn varmint at any time. Smokey the Bear looks cute on National Geographic but not when it gets into your car at three in the morning. Deer mice are endearing little furballs until you find out they are carrying the hantavirus.

A farmer I know says, "If you can kill it with a .22 shot from ten yards, it's just a varmint."

What would PETA say?

Beaver
© Robert S. Michelson/Tom Stack & Associates

Love 'em or hate 'em
By Carolyn Dufurrena

The high valley stream had downcut perhaps ten feet below the level of the meadow. "There used to be beavers here," said the sheepherder, "and there were beaver ponds all through this valley. Then there was a big water year and the beaver dams all blew out at once." The flood took the meadow with it. Several decades later, the meadow is still well above the level of the stream.

In other places, beavers have gone a long way to re-establishing the water table, causing sagebrush to die back and wet meadow grasses to reestablish. One rancher has fenced his cattle out of most of this riparian area. But this spring, a wetter than normal year, he says, the beavers have all left, perhaps seeking new territory, fresh stands of willows. What will happen when the high water builds up behind beaver dams that are no longer maintained?

Beavers build dams, and the dams create wetlands, home to fish, turtles, frogs, birds and ducks. They also gnaw down trees, shrubs and juniper fence posts, which they don't always use to build dams. Those fallen trees can clog a canyon or make a livestock trail impassable in a matter of days, not to mention what the loss of a few well-placed fence posts can accomplish. Love 'em or hate 'em, beavers are a force to be reckoned with.

The joy of fishing

These large aquatic soaring birds, white pelicans, are feeding on tui chub below Marble Bluff Dam on Nevada's Truckee River. © Larry Turner

A wood-fire branding
Haythorn Ranch crew work cattle in Arthur, Nebraska, 2004. The ground crews' horses are hobbled.
© Charles W. Guildner

Just before work
Kevin Cooksley, Cooksley Clear Creek Ranch, Berwyn, Nebraska, 2003.
© Charles W. Guildner

Camp cook

Mike Colbert on the Haythorn Ranch in Nebraska, 2002.
© Charles W. Guildner

Western gothic

Denley and Lisa Norman, with border collie Bell, at the Haythorn Ranch in western Nebraska in 1996.
© Charles W. Guildner

Tack room

Steve Cooksley in the one-room schoolhouse tack museum in Anselmo, Nebraska, 2003.
© Charles W. Guildner

Sorting sheep, two thousand head

Arambel Midlands Ranch in Boulder, Wyoming. These ewes are close to lambing. © Charles W. Guildner

A tree frog in winter

By Carolyn Dufurrena

Winters are long in the cold desert. After cows and calves are put away for the season, cowboys get antsy. There's not much for them to do all winter, and often they move on to other jobs. Mom and the kids go to town for school; Dad stays home, keeping the place going on his own: chopping ice, checking the cattle, keeping the pipes from freezing, reading stacks of books from the bookmobile.

That winter season, our son was deep into his senior year. Wrestling tournaments took us all over the state, and many weekends we didn't get home to the ranch till late Saturday night. Jesus and Juan had gone home to Mexico to visit their grandchildren, and the ranch was a quiet place, the territory of owls and coyotes and quick little herds of deer.

One morning in that two-monthlong chunk of quiet time between Christmas and calving, Tim stumbled into the cold bathroom to brush his teeth—and a frog hopped out of the sink drain. It looked just like the little green frogs that hop around the gardens and lawns all summer, except this frog wasn't green. He was yellow.

Old ranch-house plumbing is a mystery best left unsolved. Suffice to say, in the summer, frogs regularly climb up into the bathtub or the kitchen sink or the pump drain. One wet summer, one of our neighbors moved frogs out of her bathtub by the handful every day.

Unfortunately, most of them are not content to stay in the sink or the bathtub. Their nocturnal explorations take them all over the house. The lucky ones find their way onto the pale linoleum kitchen floor, or they hop in front of the TV during the evening news. Those survivors end up back on the lawn. Others are not so fortunate. We find the unsuccessful pioneers fossilized under cabinets and in the corners, covered with spiderwebs, when we sweep. But that's summer. This is January. A frog in January is an apocalyptic creature.

This little frog didn't look emaciated. In fact, except for his chlorophyll-poor shade of yellow, he was in pretty good shape. He must be eating something.

My husband is good at not fixing things that aren't broken. If a leppie calf can steal milk from another calf's mama, and if the cow will have him, he'll let them be, allowing the solutions of Nature to supersede his own. He left the little frog on the sink.

The frog was there the next day, crawling out of the trap as Tim ran the freezing cold water to brush his teeth, and he was there the day after that. After the third day, he named him Oscar. Tim and Oscar met regularly in the bathroom that winter, usually while Tim was shaving.

"What are you havin' for supper tonight, Tim?"

"Salami and Early Times, maybe some crackers. How 'bout you, Oscar?"

"Whiskers and toothpaste, probably. Maybe some dead skin."

Oscar kept Tim company all through January and February. Of course, Tim didn't say anything to me about his new friend. I came home one weekend to find Oscar in his place on the sink, not wanting to go down the drain, not wanting, particularly, to swim around in the sinkful of warm water I ran for him.

"Hey Tim," I called. "There's a frog on the sink."

"Just leave him be. He'll be fine," Tim called back from the kitchen, not willing to divulge his relationship with his amphibian pal. I wondered what on earth a frog could live on all winter in the septic system. Maybe there was a weird chemosynthesis going on down there in the leach line like those volcanic fumaroles on the ocean floor, supporting a whole biota specifically evolved to cold water and whiskers and toothpaste.

I didn't see much of a future for him, but in the winter the ranch house was Tim's territory. Whatever relationships will sustain my cowboy husband through this solitary season, I have learned to let 'em be.

Skeptically, I shut the bathroom light off. When I didn't see Oscar the next weekend, I suspected the worst. But then, of course, time passed, and I forgot about him. I should have known.

Oscar
Straight out of the drain, adorned with Tim's whiskers.
© Carolyn Dufurrena

By July, summer is in full swing. Cowboys are up and out before dawn, haying machinery rumbles through the yard at all hours of the day and night. Our dear friends come to visit with their young son, who is fascinated with the backyard wildlife. I tell him the story of Tim's winter frog. "I don't know what happened to him," I conclude. "Maybe he spent the rest of the winter in the pipes."

Tim looks a little sheepish. "Well," he confesses. "One March afternoon I turned him out on the lawn by the back door. It looked like he could use the sun. It was warm that day, and it was warm the next day, but the day after that..." He winces. "Well, I hope Oscar remembered how to dig."

The other day I walked up the back steps to find a fat yellow frog sitting on a brass hinge that used to hold a screen door. The frog was almost invisible against its yellowish green. I shooed him off onto the lawn, thinking how the frogs in the yard were really much greener than he was. And then, of course, it hit me. It was Oscar, giving Tim the message: only ninety-eight more shaving days until Christmas.

Cattle and dust
Dan Coon and the Baldauf brothers move cows and calves down the road to the sorting corrals in Wisdom, Montana. There the calves will be vaccinated and wormed prior to their weaning within the next month. © Cynthia Baldauf

Tired cow dogs
Wheeler and Dillon catch a snooze back at camp after a hard day working cows at Campwood Cattle Company's Wildhorse Ranch in Bagdad, Arizona. © Kathy McCraine

Roping

Logan Bates gets airborne as he and Dave Pawel flank a big calf. KJ Kasum, on Spook, has just dragged it to the fire at Campwood Cattle Company's winter branding pens on the 7 Up Ranch in Prescott, Arizona. © Kathy McCraine

"Sometimes, I just come out here and drive around on a Sunday morning, listening to NPR and hanging out with the girls."

Savanna "Scout" Cox Hebbert, on spending a little quality time with her Four Bar O heifers in the Nebraska Sandhills

Coffee with the ladies
Ned Thompson checks cows early in the morning in Pollok, Texas.
© Connie Thompson

Quiet time

Early morning gather
Gaiser cattle are about to move to summer grazing in the high country. Chinese Camp, California. © Terri Arington

Looking for love
During a winter storm a western mule deer buck stays with the does during the annual breeding rut. Tule Lake Basin, California.
© Larry Turner

Bringing 'em in

Time for branding on the Lavaggi Ranch in California's gold country.
© Larry Angier

Bringing him back
Dennis Mitchell chases after a calf that turned back from the rest of the herd on the Pankratz Ranch near Cleveland, Montana. © Todd Klassy

Gathering

"Every sort of life has its own zest for those who are bred to it."

Mary Austin, "The Flock," 1906

Bringing a calf to the fire
Cowgirl Colie Moline of Geraldine, Montana, cinches her rope on the Hofeldt Ranch near Lloyd, Montana. © Todd Klassy

Branding time

Caught!

Yvonne Wooster, right, gets a head loop on a frisky calf as Gary Poggio gets ready to heel during branding with Elliot Joses near Valley Springs in Calaveras County, California. The calf to the right? It's been branded and earmarked with a sharp knife, thus the bloody ear. © Larry Angier

Irons in the fire

Ropers and ground crew are at work as Elliott Joses reaches for a hot brand. This is spring branding for Loree and Doug Joses at the Levaggi Ranch in Plymouth, California.
© Robin Dell'Orto

Riding flank
Casey Mott and his dog "Dawg" trail cattle during the Nomad Cattle Company fall gather in Forsyth, Montana.
© Guy de Galard

Call the medic
Watched by mama, Matt Clark finishes doctoring her calf at a ranch in Daniel, Wyoming.
© Skye Clark

Solitude

Moving yearlings
Sandee Nelson and her cowdogs push young cows across Blacktail Ridge near Dillon, Montana.
© Susan Marxer

Soaked
Cowboy Lael Barnett, with help from horse Maddie and dog Screech, move a herd of cattle in the rain in the Bear Paw Mountains near Lloyd, Montana.
© Todd Klassy

I can't look at hobbles and I can't stand fences
A saddle horse fights its confinement during branding at the Padlock Ranch in Dayton, Wyoming.
© Guy de Galard

Jennifer's mules wear diamonds
Riding for the McGee Creek Pack Station in the Sierra Nevada, California, Jennifer Roeser brings her pack string down the McGee Creek Trail.
© Kent A. Reeves

The shaming of the cat

By Robert Laxalt, from "Sweet Promised Land," 1957

When I reached the camp, I learned that the lion had already hit the band. It had been a quiet kill, and my father had no knowledge of it until he noticed a ewe bleating lonely and searching for her lamb....

There was an evening breeze coming up, and it was in our faces, and it brought with it the occasional tinkle of a bell. Every once in a while, as we cut down through the ravines, we could catch glimpses of the sheep scattered in the meadow below.

Then, almost inaudibly, the breeze brought to us the low sound of running hoofs. My father stopped and peered down into the meadow. Abruptly, he changed our direction and began to walk to the right of the hill in front of us. At his heels, Barbo started to whimper, but my father silenced him with a quick command. I wanted to ask him what he had seen, but for some reason I had the feeling it was none of my business.

To one side of the hill in front of us, there was a narrow ravine that emptied into the meadow below. My father swung into it with his long stride, and I followed, trying to make as little sound as possible. We descended rapidly, and in a few minutes we were almost out of the ravine. My father was about twenty feet in front of me when he reached the meadow, and came face to face with the lion.

I had been looking at the ground, and the first warning I had of it was when I heard the sob in Barbo's throat. I jerked my head up and saw the lion. I remember only an odd shock at the fact of his freedom, and then my mind and my face both froze.

They must have stared at each other for full seconds. The lion cocked his head to one side, almost curiously, and rumbled once deep in his chest. Then, slowly, my father raised his *makila*, his walking stick, and began to advance toward the lion. The rumble started again, this time in ominous warning, and with that startling suddenness of motion the lion dropped into a crouch.

Even then, there was not a hint of hesitation in my father's movements. He did not falter once in his stride. His stick was still raised in the air, as though not to fend but to strike, and his pose was menacing. They were only a few feet apart when the lion, as though he had suddenly become uncertain, straightened and then crouched again, and then incredibly began to back up. And now, his neck was not rigid any more. He tossed his head, snarling and showing his fangs. And still my father pursued him in that relentless advance.

When I remember, I realize that the lion must not even have known where he was backing, because when his hindquarters met the pole fence he recoiled as if he had been burned, and in one lightning motion wheeled completely around. And when he turned to face my father again, the confusion was gone and the motion deadly. This time, his eyes were burning red and he was crouching to spring. And still my father did not pause an instant, but came toward him with his stick raised in the air.

There was a single beat of time before the lion sprang when he seemed to arrest his muscles and reset them. Afterward I could remember, but at the instant I could not understand that this had happened. When the lion left the ground, my mind had already prepared its next image, that of seeing my father go down in a blinding flurry of talons.

Mountain lion

© Tom Stack/Tom Stack & Associates

But he did not. By some feat, the lion seemed to leap directly at him, and then arch his body away so that he actually came to light at the side of my father.

And then, almost in the same motion, he began to run away. He did not bolt, but took his leave loping unhurriedly in the direction of the trees, looking back and snarling every once in a while, as though maintaining a degree of self-respect. My father did not follow him, but stood now with his stick to the ground and leaning on it a little, watching until the lion had disappeared in the trees.

When it was over I felt hot words at my lips. But then my father turned and there was a private pity in his face that had not yet fully vanished, as though now he felt sorrow at the lion's shame, and I could not say a word, because I knew then that foolhardiness had been no part of it at all.

In the spring, Janna Hampton and Alan Fulfer bring in the mares from winter pastures for the Hampton Ranch in Ten Sleep, Wyoming. © Guy de Galard

Photographers & writers

Sarah B. ANDERSON, photographer, teacher, The Dalles, Oregon. She specializes in farm and ranch photography. *sbaphotography.smugmug.com*

Larry ANGIER, photographer, Jackson, California. He is multi-award-winning and has published everywhere. He is also RANGE's webmaster. *angier-fox.photoshelter.com*

Terri ARINGTON, photographer, Columbia, California.

Cynthia BALDAUF, photographer, Pittsboro, Indiana, and Big Hole Valley, Montana. She specializes in ranch and agricultural photography. *cynthiabaldaufimages.com*

John BARDWELL, writer, artist, book designer, Reno, Nevada. He has designed all of RANGE's thirteen books and about twenty years of RANGE magazine.

Debbie BELL, photographer, Clements, California.

Marlene BELL, photographer, Big Sandy, Utah.

Virginia BENNETT, writer, poet, cowgirl, Winthrop, Washington.

Annie BRANGER, photographer, Chinook, Montana. *annieophotos.com*

Cathy BROWN, photographer, Grass Valley, Oregon.

Eberhard BRUNNER, photographer, Anchorage, Alaska. He is a retired Alpine ski racer and well-known bush pilot who spends his time between Alaska and Africa. His picture of a cheetah family won National Geographic's prestigious Grand Prize. *eberhardbrunnerphotography.com*

Terri BUTLER, photographer, Wellington, Nevada (deceased). She was a regular at "Shooting the West" and took many pictures of western people, wildlife and landscapes.

Skye CLARK, photographer, rancher, Smoot, Wyoming.

Jim CUNNINGHAM, photographer, LeGrand, California.

Jennifer DeFREECE, photographer, ranch mom, Casper, Wyoming.

Guy de GALARD, photographer, Buffalo, Wyoming. He runs "Cowboy Adventures," which provides a real western experience for French travelers.

Robin DELL'ORTO, photographer, rancher, Mokelumne, California.

Marion DICKINSON, photographer, rancher, Greybull, Wyoming.

Carolyn DUFURRENA, writer, Denio, Nevada. She is the author of "Fifty Miles From Home: Riding the Long Circle on a Nevada Family Ranch." She has contributed to many anthologies and performs regularly at the National Cowboy Poetry Gathering in Elko, Nevada. *carolyndufurrena.wordpress.com*

John DUFURRENA, writer, Boise, Idaho.

Linda DUFURRENA, photographer, rancher, Denio, Nevada. Her award-winning book, "Fifty Miles from Home," is in its fourth printing. *lindadufurrena.com*

Gerri DUKE, photographer, Cañon City, Colorado.

Valerie DUTTER, photographer, Carson City, Nevada.

Willie FELTON, photographer, Ten Sleep, Wyoming.

Tim FINDLEY, writer, Fallon, Nevada (deceased). He was a brilliant investigative reporter for the San Francisco Chronicle, Rolling Stone, and RANGE magazine. He was the adopted son of Adam Fortunate Eagle Nordwall, whom he met while covering the Alcatraz occupation, and was made an honorary Crow.

Robin L. GREEN, photographer, Moses Lake, Washington. Her work centers on farm and ranch subjects. *thebaymare.com*

Carol GRENIER, photographer, Carson City, Nevada.

Charles W. GUILDNER, photographer, writer, Everett, Washington. His "Lives of Tradition" negatives are archived at the Great Plains Art Museum in Lincoln, Nebraska. His work is in several permanent museum collections, including the Museum of Nebraska Art and the Joslyn Art Museum. *guildner-photo.com*

Linda HAMMOND, photographer, rancher, Fallon, Nevada.

Alan HART, photographer, writer, gypsy moth trapper, surveyor, Troutdale, Virginia.

"When the ranch is in peace, no other life is more perfect."

Charles Goodnight (1836-1929), Texas rancher

Linda M. **HASSELSTROM**, writer, Hermosa, South Dakota. Rancher and Wrangler award-winning cowboy poet and essayist, author of fourteen books. Her blog, "Notes from a Western Life," can be found at *windbreakhouse.wordpress.com.*

Mark **HAYWARD**, photographer, Lamoille, Nevada. He won "Best of Show" in RANGE's 2009 Outback Roundup photo contest. *haywardwildlife.com*

Jon **HILL**, photographer, Yerington, Nevada.

Chris **HOLLOWAY**, photographer, Post Falls, Idaho. His passion is capturing light and spirit. *bychrisphotography.smugmug.com*

Tammy L. **HOOVER**, photographer, Evanston, Wyoming. She specializes in wildlife and nature.

Sheree **JENSEN**, photographer, Fallon, Nevada. *shereejensenphotography.com*

Janet **JOHNSON**, photographer, Denio, Nevada.

Bill **JONES**, writer, New Tazewell, Tennessee. He has a small farm with fifty cows, three horses, and two lazy bulls, and writes cowboy poetry. He is working on a memoir of the Vietnam War.

David **KIMBLE**, photographer, Spring Creek, Nevada.

Todd **KLASSY**, photographer, Havre, Montana. He specializes in farm and ranch photography. He won the International Federation of Agricultural Journalists Star Prize for Photography in 2016, the first American to win in fouteen years. *toddklassy.com*

Robert **LAXALT**, writer, Reno, Nevada (deceased). A prolific, Pulitzer-prize-nominated author who documented the lives of Basques in the West. He founded the University of Nevada Press and helped start the Basque Studies program at UNR.

Jessica Brandi **LIFLAND**, photographer, San Francisco, California. She has published in the New York Times, USA Today, and Via Magazine, and is the official photographer for the National Cowboy Poetry Gathering in Elko, Nevada. *jess@jessicalifland.com*

Carol **LISTER**, photographer, El Dorado Hills, California.

Rene **MAESTREJUAN**, writer, educator, Jordan Valley, Oregon.

Susan **MARXER**, photographer, Twin Bridges, Montana. *no-ruby.wix.com/saddlescenes*

Diane **McALLISTER**, photographer, Reno, Nevada. Her work has been featured in magazines, calendars, and in National Wildlife Federation's "Wild Animal Baby." *imprintsofnature.com*

Caitlyn **McCOLLUM**, photographer, Rozet, Wyoming.

Kathy **McCRAINE**, writer, photographer, Prescott, Arizona. She is the author of "Ranch Album," "The Romance of Western Life," and "Cow Country Cooking: Recipes and Tales From Northern Arizona's Historic Ranches." *kathymccraine.com*

Duane **McGARVA**, photographer, rancher, Likely, California. *wheretheweststilllives.com*

Rebekah G. **MENDENHALL**, photographer, Haines, Alaska.

Bruce **MOST**, photographer, Denver, Colorado.

Patricia **NEELY**, photographer, Susanville, California.

James **PLOYHAR**, writer, rancher, Great Falls, Montana, raises grain and native seed with his brother.

Sandy **POWELL**, photographer, Coleville, California.

Cindy **QUIGLEY**, photographer, Oroville, California. Her work is featured in "Go West: The Risk and the Reward," published by Range Conservation Foundation and RANGE magazine. *cmqphotography.smugmug.com*

Vess **QUINLAN**, writer, farmer, rancher, cowboy poet, Florence, Colorado. He performs regularly at the National Cowboy Poetry Gathering in Elko, Nevada.

Kent A. **REEVES**, photographer, conservationist, cowboy, Sacramento, California.

Jennifer **ROBERTS**, photographer, Daniel, Wyoming.

Millie **ROESCH**, photographer, Guernsey, Wyoming.

Kayla **SARGENT**, photographer, Shawmut, Montana.

Chrystal **SIMS**, photographer, Evanston, Wyoming.

Jurij **STRUTYNSKY**, photographer, Grass Valley, California.

Ozana **STURGEON**, photographer, Woodland Park, Colorado. She is an equine photographer and mixed-media artist. *ozanaphotography.com*

Connie **THOMPSON**, photographer, writer, rancher, Pollok, Texas.

Sandy **TIBBALS**, photographer, Fernley, Nevada.

Andrea **TOLMAN**, photographer, Basin, Wyoming.

TOM STACK & ASSOC., Tavernier, Florida. A leading supplier of extraordinary and hard-to-find wildlife, underwater, space and environmental images worldwide. TSA photographers in this book include **Scott Linstead, Joe McDonald, Robert S. Michelson, Terrence Ross, Therisa Stack,** and **Tom Stack**. *tomstackassociates.photoshelter.com*

Larry **TURNER**, photographer, Malin, Oregon. His work has appeared in National Geographic Traveler, Gourmet, Sunset, and Travel & Leisure. *larryturnerphotography.com*

Sarah E. **WAGONER**, photographer, Rural Retreat, Virginia.

Pam **WHITE**, photographer, Snowflake, Arizona, and Jordan Valley, Oregon. She is a rancher and "Grammy" to the next generation and she always packs her camera and her lipstick.

Pamela S. **WICKKISER**, photographer, Winnemucca, Nevada.

"Riding a horse isn't what it looks like: it isn't a person sitting in a saddle telling the horse what to do by yanking on the reins. Real riding is a lot like ballroom dancing or maybe figure skating in pairs. It's a relationship."

Temple Grandin, "Animals in Translation," 2006

A cold ride
Tom Bercher on High Lonesome on a winter evening in Wyoming.
© Carol Grenier